Unafraid
Youth Leader Guide

Unafraid:
Living with Courage and Hope in Uncertain Times

Unafraid
978-1-5247-6033-5 *Hardcover*
978-1-5247-6034-2 *e-Book*

Unafraid: DVD
978-1-5018-5375-3

Unafraid: Leader Guide
978-1-5018-5373-9
978-1-5018-5374-6 *e-Book*

Unafraid: Youth Leader Guide
978-1-5018-5382-1
978-1-5018-5383-8 *e-Book*

Unafraid: Children's Leader Guide
978-1-5018-5384-5

Also from Adam Hamilton

24 Hours That Changed the World	*Making Sense of the Bible*
Christianity and World Religions	*Moses*
Christianity's Family Tree	*Not a Silent Night*
Confronting the Controversies	*Revival*
Creed	*Seeing Gray in a World of Black and White*
Enough	*Selling Swimsuits in the Arctic*
Faithful	*Speaking Well*
Final Words from the Cross	*The Call*
Forgiveness	*The Journey*
Half Truths	*The Way*
John	*Unleashing the Word*
Leading Beyond the Walls	*When Christians Get It Wrong*
Love to Stay	*Why?*

For more information, visit www.AdamHamilton.org.

UNAFRAID

LIVING WITH

COURAGE AND HOPE IN

UNCERTAIN TIMES

ADAM HAMILTON

Youth Leader Guide
by Josh Tinley

Abingdon Press / Nashville

Unafraid
Living with Courage and Hope in Uncertain Times
Youth Leader Guide

This book is printed on elemental chlorine-free paper.

ISBN 978-1-5018-5382-1

18 19 20 21 22 23 24 25 26 27 — 10 9 8 7 6 5 4 3 2 1
MANUFACTURED IN THE UNITED STATES OF AMERICA

CONTENTS

INTRODUCTION

From *Unafraid*, by Adam Hamilton

One of the most repeated instructions in the Bible is "Don't be afraid." These words, in one form or another, appear over 140 times in scripture. They remind us that ordinary women and men from the age of Israel's patriarchs to first-century Christians struggled with fear. But they also show us that faith can be pivotal to overcoming fear and finding peace in uncertain times.

In one way or another, all of us are afraid. We fear the future. We fear each other. We fear death. Fear can be good. It can be useful. It can protect us. But if fear is not warranted, it can harm us and others, and it can prevent us from becoming the people God intends for us to be. How can we deal with our fears? How can we manage our fears and perhaps even overcome them?

Pastor and author Adam Hamilton takes a thoughtful, inspiring look at these questions in his book *Unafraid: Living with Courage and Hope in Uncertain Times*. The book will be of interest to both adults and young people. With the latter audience in mind, we are offering this Youth Leader Guide.

The guide is designed for flexible use by youth groups in a five-session study. It is perfect for youth groups that are reading Adam Hamilton's book and would like a leader guide geared to young people. Alternatively, since this guide makes extensive use of quotations from Adam Hamilton's book, it can be used as a self-contained study, in which each youth group member has a copy to read and refer to.

How the Guide Is Organized

This study will explore the subject of fear, as presented in Adam Hamilton's book *Unafraid*. The book consists of five parts, each made up of four chapters. This Youth Leader Guide is structured accordingly, for ease of use with the book—five sessions with four activities each, one activity per book chapter.

Each session begins with a summary of the material in that part of the book, followed by an opening activity, the four chapter activities, and a closing activity with prayer. Estimated times are given for each activity, with the total being roughly one hour. Groups can tailor the times and activities to fit the needs of their particular group.

Blessings to you and your group as you begin to explore *Unafraid: Living with Courage and Hope in Uncertain Times*.

1

UNDERSTANDING AND COUNTERING FEAR

Fear is a universal human condition. We all know what it feels like to be afraid. Sometimes fear can protect us from harm. The fear of pain and injury may keep us from touching a hot stove or jumping off a second-story balcony; the fear of being grounded may inspire us to keep up with our schoolwork and study for the next big test.

But fear also can be destructive. A fear of failure or rejection or getting hurt can keep us from taking advantage of opportunities; it can make us reluctant to take risks and make sacrifices; it can prevent us from answering God's call or taking a stand for people who are suffering.

In Part One of his book *Unafraid: Living with Courage and Hope in Uncertain Times*, pastor and author Adam Hamilton explores what fear is and where it comes from. He looks at how fear can be a gift and how fear can cause brokenness and suffering. Hamilton also discusses how we—as children of God and followers of Christ—face our fears and respond to fear with faith.

This session corresponds to the following chapters in *Unafraid* by Adam Hamilton:

- Chapter 1: Afraid
- Chapter 2: The Anatomy of Fear
- Chapter 3: Paralyzed by Fear a Mile from the Promised Land
- Chapter 4: Facing Your Fears

Session Activities

Opening: Hopes and Fears (5–10 minutes)

Supplies: whiteboard or paper, markers

From *Unafraid*, by Adam Hamilton

The reality is everyone worries about something. We all have things we fear. And most of us will have seasons when anxieties and fear simply overwhelm us. Fear is a powerful emotion that shapes all of us in profound ways we often don't fully understand. Look behind depression's door, and you'll often find fear. Addictions, too. Peer beneath broken marriages and friendships, beneath prejudice and hate, and you'll find fear.

Often during worship and fellowship, Christian communities share joys and concerns. Joys are praises and things that people are thankful for; concerns are worries and situations in need of healing. To open your time together, exchange joys and concerns but, for purposes of this study, use the language of "hopes" and "fears."

For example: "My grandparents are visiting, and I hope that we will have a good time together." "I fear that a friend of mine is hurting because of some family problems." List these hopes and fears on a whiteboard or large sheet of paper.

Open your time together with this prayer or one of your own:

God, as we prepare to begin this study, we give you our hopes and our fears. We thank you for all the ways that you have blessed us and the hope that we have through you. We ask for the strength and courage to face and endure our fears. Watch over us during this time together, that we will learn about ourselves and our faith and grow in our relationships with one another and with you. Amen.

Afraid (10–15 minutes)

Supplies: whiteboard or paper, markers

From *Unafraid*, by Adam Hamilton

Often we fear things that will never happen; yet real or imagined, these fears have power. Sometimes our battles with fear take a more serious turn, becoming a debilitating struggle with panic attacks or anxiety disorders. There are other times when fear is well placed, and people have good reason to be afraid: they are facing life-threatening illnesses, the impending death of a loved one, potentially devastating legal conflicts, or significant economic distress.

Each person in the group should jot down in the space below a list of his or her top five fears. Participants need not be too specific. Allow a few minutes for everyone to create a list. Ask each person to read aloud the list of fears. Discuss:

Have someone read aloud the selection from *Unafraid* by Adam Hamilton that's shown above. Hamilton argues that fear is behind many of the problems we face as individuals, communities, and nations, including problems of depression, addiction, prejudice, and violence. Write those four words across the top of a whiteboard or large sheet of paper. Ask:

- What fears might cause each of the four things shown on the board?

As fears are named, list them under the result they might lead to. For instance, someone might say, "Fear of failure." Consider whether a fear of failure could result in depression or addiction or prejudice or violence; then list it under the appropriate heading or headings. Spend about five minutes brainstorming fears. Then ask:

- How has fear had bad consequences for you?

Adam Hamilton says that fears have power. Sometimes fear is justified and protects us from dangerous situations. But often fear is painful and destructive. To counteract the power of fear, we need to take a look at what fear is and what tools God gives us to deal with it.

The Anatomy of Fear (15 minutes)

Supplies: note cards, markers, Bibles

From *Unafraid*, by Adam Hamilton

Our body's capacity to experience fear, and our ability to respond to perceived threats, when working properly, are absolutely amazing. ... Your heart begins to race, your breathing becomes more rapid and more shallow, your mouth gets dry, your muscles tense up—all aimed at helping you fight or flee. ... Our responses to a perceived danger happen almost instantaneously—before the rational mind can process the experience.

Have each participant write on a note card the name of an animal. The animals chosen should be well-known animals that everyone in the group would be familiar with.

Collect the animal cards. Have one person shuffle them and hand them out to the members of the group. Allow everyone a minute to think about how the animal on the card would react when threatened in a "fight-or-flight" situation. Would the animal on the card lunge and attack? Would it roll into a ball? Would it turn and run away? One at a time, allow each person to mimic how that particular animal would act in such a situation.

Then brainstorm a list of threats that might cause a young person to make a flight-or-fight response. These can be situations where a person feels physically threatened, emotionally threatened, or placed under a great deal of stress. Discuss:

- In which of these situations would you fight? ("Fighting" doesn't necessarily mean swinging fists or exchanging harsh words; it just means actively confronting the threat.)
- In which of these situations would you flee? (Again, "fleeing" isn't limited to literally running away but would include any effort to avoid confrontation.)
- In what sorts of situations is it better to confront a threat?
- In what sorts of situations is it better to walk away from a threat?

Read aloud each of the Scripture passages below. For each one, discuss:

- What threat do people in the story encounter?
- How do they respond to this threat—by fight or by flight?
- What do you think is the appropriate response in this situation?

Scriptures:

- Numbers 13:25–14:10
- John 18:1-12

13

Fear is a gift from God that helps us avoid danger. But, as Adam Hamilton points out, "we often misread signals, worry about threats that are not real, and find ourselves overwhelmed by false fears, paralyzing anxiety, or unhealthy fretting concerning things that (a) we don't need to be afraid of, (b) will never happen, or (c) worrying and fear can do nothing to save us from." The rest of this study will look at how we can face and overcome these destructive fears.

Paralyzed by Fear a Mile from the Promised Land (10 minutes)

Supplies: Bibles, paper, pens or pencils

From *Unafraid*, by Adam Hamilton
Before entering the land, the Israelites sent twelve spies. ... Two of the spies said, in effect, "It's all there, just like God promised. And it's awesome! God is with us—let's go get it!" But then the other ten spies spoke up. "We can't go and take the land," they said. "The city walls are strong, the people are even stronger. They look like the giants of old. ..."

And with that, the same people who had witnessed God's deliverance from the mighty Egyptians began to weep and suggest it was time to give up. ... It wasn't until the next generation arose that the children of Israel finally entered the Promised Land. Can you imagine, for thirty-eight years they remained paralyzed by fear just a mile from the Promised Land.

Discuss:

- When has fear kept you from trying something or taking advantage of an opportunity?
- You looked at the story from Numbers 13–14 as a part of the previous activity. Do you think that the Israelites' fear in this Scripture was justified? Why or why not?
- What did the Israelites lose out on because they gave in to fear?

- In this situation, the people of Israel showed a lack of faith. What does it mean to have faith in something or someone?

Whenever there is a major tragedy, such as a natural disaster or act of violence, prominent figures respond by offering thoughts and prayers. As Christians we believe that prayer is an effective and necessary response to tragedy. We also believe that a faithful response to any situation requires not only prayer but also action.

Divide into teams of three or four. Have each team come up with a seemingly impossible situation or insurmountable challenge, like the giants that the Israelites faced in the Promised Land. Teams should try to come up with situations that are relevant right now (such as issues facing your community or recent disasters that have been in the news).

Once a team has selected a situation, it should come up with a prayer and a plan of action:

- Prayer: Teams should write a prayer that (a) lifts up the struggles that people are facing, (b) thanks God for those who are working to heal the situation, and (c) asks God to offer strength and comfort both to those affected and those helping.
- Plan of Action: Teams should come up with one specific way to bring healing to the situation. As needed, do research to learn what the real needs are and what efforts are already under way to address the situation. It is also quite possible that the best way to help is to donate money. (Most food banks, for example, prefer cash donations to food donations because they know what food is most needed and are able to purchase large amounts of food for little money.) If this is the case, come up with a plan for raising the money that you will donate.

Spend about ten minutes working on prayers and plans of action. Then have each team read its prayer and summarize its plan. As a group, determine one plan to follow through on. Decide what your next steps will be and who will be responsible for these steps. Then discuss:

- How can the prayers and plans of action you came up with bring hope to people and communities experiencing fear?
- Why is it important to respond with both prayer and a plan of action?
- How does having a plan of action keep us from being paralyzed by fear and giving up in the face of adversity?

Facing Your Fears (10 minutes)

Supplies: Bibles

From *Unafraid*, by Adam Hamilton

My daughter Danielle ... while enrolled at Kansas State University ... joined the skydiving club. ... I asked her why in the world she would do something like that, and she said, "Dad, I joined the skydiving club as a way of confronting all of life's fears head-on, in one act. I knew that in my family I was genetically predisposed to anxiety, and I wanted to take preventative measures to keep fear from being a governing force in my life."

Refer back to the fears you listed for the activity called "Afraid." Discuss:

- When have you had to face one of these fears? (In other words, when have you had to do something you were afraid of doing, such as speaking in public or flying or dealing with a spider?)
- Have you, like Danielle, benefited by confronting your fear?

Some version of the words "fear" or "afraid" appear more than 400 times in the Bible, and the most common phrase in the Bible is (depending on translation), "Do not be afraid." Read aloud Luke 1:26-38. Ask:

- Who is told not to be afraid? What might she have to fear?
- How does the person in this Scripture face her fear?

Adam Hamilton says, "We can focus our imagination on all the things that might happen, and by inflating the threats or obstacles we face, we turn them into giants. Or we can focus our imagination on the presence of God … and trust that we will sense his love and mercy holding us near. When we imagine God's presence and power we find we can begin to live with courage and hope."

- How do you see courage and hope in play in Luke 1:26-38?

Closing (5 minutes)

Close your time together by discussing the following questions:

- What is one thing that you learned or that you will think about differently as a result of today's session?
- What is one thing that you will do this week in response to what you've learned or discussed today?

Close with the prayer below or one of your own:

God of faith and hope, thank you for this time we've had to reflect on our fears and imagine how we can bring healing and comfort to those who are suffering and afraid. Watch over us this week, and guide us to be people who put our faith into action. Amen.

2

CRIME, RACE, TERRORISM, AND POLITICS

One of humankind's most common and deadly fears is the fear of one another. We worry about violent crime and acts of terror; we feel threatened by people with different worldviews or different perspectives on issues that we care about. These fears can lead to prejudice and hate. We assume that certain groups of people are dangerous based on the actions of a few of their members; we become suspicious of people whose cultures and points of view we don't understand.

In Part Two of his book *Unafraid: Living With Courage and Hope in Uncertain Times*, pastor and author Adam Hamilton looks at how and why we fear people of different cultural backgrounds, religious beliefs, and political views and at how these fears spread and become destructive. He also considers how we can overcome these fears and show God's love to people we might otherwise fear.

This session corresponds to the following chapters in *Unafraid* by Adam Hamilton:

- Chapter 5: We Need a Security System
- Chapter 6: Troost Avenue
- Chapter 7: Weaponizing Fear
- Chapter 8: The Sky Is Falling!

Session Activities

Opening: Hopes and Fears (5–10 minutes)

Supplies: whiteboard or paper, markers

From *Unafraid*, by Adam Hamilton

The impalas reminded me of humans. Like them, we often live on edge—never quite sure who is friend or foe, or from which direction the next threat is likely to come. But there's a big difference. The predators we fear most are not other species but our fellow human beings.

As you did in the opening session, begin your time together by sharing hopes and fears. Again, list these hopes and fears on a whiteboard or large sheet of paper.

Also use this time to discuss the plan of action you developed last week in "Paralyzed by Fear a Mile from the Promised Land." Talk about what changes you may need to make to your plan, and determine what steps you need to take next. Discuss:

- Based on the quote above from Adam Hamilton, what topics do you think might we be talking about during this session?

Then open your time together with this prayer or one of your own:

God, thank you again for this opportunity to gather together and reflect on the message you have for us. Open our hearts and minds so that we are able to let go of our fears and prejudices and see people through your eyes. As we discuss our fears and worries, remind us of the hope we have through you. Amen.

We Need a Security System (10–15 minutes)

Supplies: Bibles

From *Unafraid,* by Adam Hamilton

In a recent Gallup poll, 53 percent of Americans reported that they worry "a great deal" about crime and violence. This was up from just 39 percent two years before, and was the highest level since 2001. ... But the facts about violent crime are quite different from our fears. ... Violent crime rates have reduced by more than half since the early 1990s, and the murder rate has dropped to the level it was in 1964.

Adam Hamilton, in *Unafraid,* says that television shows featuring violent crime, as well as twenty-four-hour news coverage on television and social media, have caused people to be very frightened of violent crime, even though crime rates are historically low. Discuss:

- For what other reasons might people be afraid of violent crime?
- Hamilton points out that, statistically, one's chances of being a victim of violent crime are very slim. What are you afraid of, even though you are statistically unlikely to be hurt by it?

Though many of the things we fear are unlikely to affect us, there are certainly times when fear is justified. Regardless of what we fear or why we are afraid, we should not allow our fears to control us or cause us to act impulsively. We can avoid giving in to fear by releasing our fears to God. One way to surrender to God and to experience God's assurance is through a practice called *lectio divina,* or "divine reading."

Lectio divina involves taking a short passage of Scripture, reading it slowly, and meditating on it while listening for God's voice. Try this method of prayer using Psalm 27:1, 14.

> *The LORD is my light and my salvation—*
>> *whom shall I fear?*
> *The LORD is the stronghold of my life—*
>> *of whom shall I be afraid? . . .*
>
> *Wait for the LORD;*
>> *be strong and take heart*
>> *and wait for the LORD.*
>
> *(NIV)*

- Select four people to read aloud this Scripture, and have everyone, except the first reader, close their eyes.
- The first reader should slowly read aloud the above verses, pausing at the end of lines. Participants should clear their minds and listen. This reading should be followed by a time of silence when participants listen for what God might be saying to them through the passage.
- After a minute or more of silence the second reader should read the passage slowly and with appropriate pauses. During the second reading participants should pay attention to what single word stands out to them the most. Following this reading, participants should spend a minute in silence reflecting on this word and what God might be saying to them through this word.
- The third reader should then slowly read aloud the Scripture. This time participants should open their minds to how God might be calling them to respond to the message of the Scripture. Allow a minute for reflection after the Scripture is read.
- The fourth reader should do one final reading. Participants need not focus on any one thing; they should just relax and hear the words one more time.

Following this experience, discuss:

- What word stood out to you during the second reading? What do you think God was saying to you through that word?
- How did God call you to respond to this Scripture?
- What does this Scripture have to say about how we respond to fear?
- What are your thoughts on this method of prayer and reading the Scriptures? What did you like? What did you not like?
- Why is it important for us to have times of silence and reflection?
- How might this method of prayer help you deal with your fears?

Lectio divina is just one way for us to turn away from our fears—particularly fears that aren't grounded in reality—and focus on God's message for our lives.

Troost Avenue (10–15 minutes)

Supplies: Bibles, pens or pencils or markers, note cards

From *Unafraid*, by Adam Hamilton

The street in Kansas City that serves as the dividing line between predominantly white and black communities is Troost Avenue. ... I grew up learning that it was not safe for a white kid like me to venture east of Troost. ... Kids like me could be robbed, beaten, or even killed "over there."

Rev. Dr. Emanuel Cleaver III grew up in the same era, just a few years behind me, but on the other side of Troost Avenue. ... Pastor Cleaver told me that sometime during his years growing up he'd picked up that it wasn't safe for black kids to be in the community where I'd been raised. He and his friends thought they could be arrested, beaten, or killed.

Discuss:

- Adam Hamilton, in *Unafraid*, says that he was raised not to be prejudiced. But he still ended up getting the impression that he should fear certain people. Why and how do you think he got this impression?

- Hamilton recalls living in a segregated area and growing up with the feeling that a nearby mostly black neighborhood was dangerous. He later got to know a pastor, Emanuel Cleaver, who had grown up in that neighborhood. Cleaver had been raised with the understanding that Hamilton's mostly white neighborhood was unsafe. What does this story tell us about the people we're taught to fear?
- Why do you think we fear people based on superficial factors such as skin color or where a person lives?
- How have you been guilty of buying into or passing along these fears?

Each person should think of a group of people and write the name of this group on a note card. These groups should not be based on race, ethnicity, religion, gender, sexuality, or any other factor that traditionally divides people. Instead groups might include, "rabbit owners," "*SpongeBob SquarePants* fans," "badminton players," or "people who only listen to music from the 1990s."

Have one person collect the cards, shuffle them, and redistribute them. Each person should come up with an absurd reason to fear the group on the card. For instance, "Rabbits are known for having more children than they can care for; rabbit owners are just enabling this irresponsible behavior and cannot be trusted." Or, "I'm OK with hitting a ball with a racket, but only someone with violent tendencies would swat at something called a 'birdie.' Badminton players are dangerous."

Allow a couple minutes for everyone to work, then see who has the most absurd reason to fear a group of people. Discuss:

- What absurd reasons do we come up with for fearing groups of people?

Read aloud each of the Scriptures below. For each one, discuss:

- What does this Scripture have to say about our attitudes toward people whom we might be taught to fear?

Scriptures:

- Acts 10:34-36
- James 2:1-4

Like Adam Hamilton in his neighborhood on one side of Troost Avenue, we all grow up in places and situations where prejudice takes hold of us. God calls us in the Scriptures to confront these prejudices and consider all people valuable children of God.

Weaponizing Fear (10 minutes)

Supplies: Bibles

From *Unafraid*, by Adam Hamilton

Something happens when you actually get to know people you might otherwise have been afraid of. More often than not, your fears disappear and your suspicions fade. You find you have empathy and compassion for them. Ideally, you make new friends.

Discuss:

- On a scale from 0 to 10, with 0 being "not at all" and 10 being "a lot," how much do you fear terrorism?
- What do you know about ISIS, Al Qaeda, or other terrorist organizations?
- In what situations do you fear terrorism the most?

As Adam Hamilton notes in *Unafraid*, we often judge entire groups—in the case of Muslims, a group of more than a billion people—based on the actions of their worst members or associates. Some people assume, because many prominent terrorists have been Muslims, that Muslims in general support violence. In reality, most Muslims are opposed to these groups, and a Muslim is far more likely to be a victim of terror than to be a terrorist.

The prejudices we see today toward Muslims and other groups also were a problem in biblical times. Read John 4:4-17, 27-30. Discuss:

- What prejudices are at play in this Scripture?
- How does Jesus respond to this prejudice?
- It was unusual for Jesus, a Jewish man, to associate with a Samaritan woman. There was a lot of tension between Jews and Samaritans, and there were taboos about men meeting with women. How did the characters in this Scripture benefit from Jesus breaking the rules and talking to the Samaritan woman?

Jesus saw the Samaritan woman not just as a Samaritan or a woman but as a person. He talked to her. He got to know her. As a result, the differences separating Jews and Samaritans became less significant. Discuss:

- How has getting to know certain people helped you overcome fear and prejudice?

Terror and panic cause us to fear people who are different from us and to assume the worst about entire groups and nations of people. Relationships enable us to overcome these fears and see others as Jesus sees them.

The Sky Is Falling! (10 minutes)

From *Unafraid*, by Adam Hamilton

When I was four or five, my parents read me a little book called *Henny Penny*. . . . In the version I read growing up, a hen named Henny Penny is scratching at the ground one day when an acorn falls on her head. Startled, she declares, "The sky is FALLING!" and runs off to tell the king. Along the way she meets her friends—a rooster, a goose, a duck, and a turkey—

and she tells each one that the sky is falling. Each in turn is seized by fear, and a kind of animal hysteria breaks loose.

Discuss:

- Are you familiar with the story of Henny Penny? What do you think is the moral of this story?
- When have you been afraid of something that turned out to be a rumor or exaggeration?
- When have you been guilty of spreading fear?

In *Unafraid*, Adam Hamilton writes about how political campaigns use fear to win votes. This strategy can be effective because, according to research done by sociologist Shana Gadarian, "when people are anxious, they tend to seek out information from sources that actually reinforce their anxiety." In other words, someone who sincerely believes that oboe players are dangerous and want to destroy our culture will probably follow Twitter accounts and cable news personalities who have similar negative views of oboe players. (This example is meant to be humorous, but you could easily imagine someone replacing "oboe players" with a race, ethnicity, religious group, or political party.) Discuss:

- From what sources do you get your information? (This would include social media accounts, television programs, podcasts, websites, and so forth.)
- On a scale from 0 to 10, where 0 is "I seek out sources of information that never agree with me on anything" and 10 is "I only seek out sources of information that completely agree with me," how would you rate the sources you turn to for information? (This would include not only sources relating to news and politics but also to entertainment, sports, games, or any other topics you may be interested in.)
- How can only reading or listening to a certain point of view feed our fears or turn us against entire groups of people?

- When have you read or heard a report that caused you to blow something out of proportion or become outraged about something you probably shouldn't have been outraged about?
- What are the benefits of listening to opposing points of view and getting information from sources you might otherwise want to avoid? How might listening to other perspectives keep you from giving in to fear?

In the previous activity, you read John 4:4-17, 27-30. Jesus, his disciples, the Samaritan woman, and those who lived in the woman's village lived in a culture that taught them to fear one another. Jesus taught them to consider a different perspective.

Take a few minutes to think about something you could do in the coming week to better understand another point of view. You could make a point of talking to someone with different religious beliefs or a different political perspective. You might take time to read or listen to a source that you would otherwise avoid. Or you could make an effort to learn about a group or culture toward which you have prejudices.

After a few minutes, find a partner and talk about the idea with your partner. Take time to listen to your partner's idea as well. Commit to holding each other accountable for following through with your ideas in the coming week. Check in with each other during the week and offer each other encouragement.

There will be times in our lives when we feel as though the sky is falling and everything is coming apart. In such times, we need to consider different perspectives and get a better understanding of what is truly happening.

Closing (5 minutes)

From *Unafraid*, by Adam Hamilton

God is our refuge and strength, a help always near in times of great trouble. That's why we won't be afraid when the world falls apart. (Psalm 46:1-2a CEB)

Close your time together by discussing the following questions:

- What is one thing that you learned from today's session or that you will think differently about as a result of today's session?
- What is one thing that you will do this week in response to what you've learned or discussed today?

Close with the prayer below or one of your own:

God, thank you for this opportunity we've had to learn from one another and from you. Make us aware, in the days and weeks to come, of how our fears divide us and cause us to be suspicious of other people. Allow us to see other people as you do and to overcome fear with love and understanding. Amen.

3

FAILURE,
DISAPPOINTING OTHERS,
INSIGNIFICANCE,
AND LONELINESS

Our culture celebrates people who take chances and try new things, but it is also quick to lash out at people who fall short of our expectations. Our fears of failure and letting other people down not only can keep us from stepping out and taking risks but also can keep us from doing things that we enjoy or are good at. These fears can keep us from being the people whom God wants us and calls us to be.

As we strive to overcome these fears, we must demonstrate love and encouragement so that others don't succumb to feelings of failure, disappointment, and loneliness. We need to recognize and remind the world that greatness isn't about what we achieve but how we demonstate love, compassion, and companionship. We must show, through our actions, that there is no reason to fear failure or loneliness, because we are surrounded by people who build us up and recognize our value.

This session corresponds to the following chapters in *Unafraid* by Adam Hamilton:

- Chapter 9: "But What If I Fail?"
- Chapter 10: Desperate to Please
- Chapter 11: Meaningless
- Chapter 12: Alone and Unloved

Session Activities

Opening: Hopes and Fears (5–10 minutes)

Supplies: whiteboard or paper, markers

From *Unafraid*, by Adam Hamilton

The fear of failure—along with all the awful accompanying scenarios we imagine of shame, the inability to provide for ourselves and those we love, and the stigma of losing—is one of the most prevalent of human fears.

As you did in the opening session, begin your time together by sharing hopes and fears. Again, list these hopes and fears on a whiteboard or large sheet of paper.

Also use this time to discuss your goal from "The Sky Is Falling!" activity from the previous session. Talk about whether you were successful. If you were not, could you follow through on your idea this week? Discuss:

- Based on the quote above from Adam Hamilton, what do you think we might be talking about during this session?

Then open your time together with this prayer or one of your own:

God, thank you again for this chance to continue examining our fears and reflecting on how we can be faithful followers of Christ. Show us how we can overcome the fear of failure and disappointment with love, compassion, and encouragement. We pray these things in Jesus' name. Amen.

"But What If I Fail?" (15 minutes)

Supplies: Bibles, a deck of cards

From *Unafraid,* by Adam Hamilton

In Luke's Gospel, Jesus spoke of "counting the cost." We must practice wise discernment as we seek to pursue a path that requires risk taking. I tend to ask questions like these: "Am I sure this is the right thing to do?" "What are the likely outcomes, both good and bad?" "Does the good accomplished justify the risk taken?" But here's an important life lesson—to live is to risk. If you always choose the risk-free, completely safe, and convenient path in life, you'll find the failure you experience is the failure to truly live.

Discuss:

- What is the biggest risk you've taken? What did you give up or risk losing?
- For what reasons might people be unwilling to take risks?
- Read the above quote from Adam Hamilton. How do we fail to "truly live" when we avoid taking risks?

Play a round or two of this simple card game that involves risk. The game begins with all participants standing. A leader has a shuffled deck of cards, which he or she will play one at a time. The object of the game is to be standing as long as possible but not to be standing when the leader plays an ace. Each time a card is played, every participant who is standing gets a point. These points accumulate. When an ace is played, the people who are still standing lose all the points they have accumulated. Players may choose to sit at any time to avoid being up when an ace is played.

Play a few rounds, add up points, and declare a winner. Then discuss:

- How did you decide how long to remain standing and when to sit?
- What risk did you take by continuing to stand?
- How would players fare in this game if they were unwilling to take risks?

To succeed in this game you must take risks. The only way to accumulate points is to remain standing, even though there's a chance that you will lose everything. Discuss:

- What could you lose, not in the game but in your life, if you were unwilling to take risks?
- How does fear of failure keep us from taking risks?
- Read Ephesians 5:15-17. What do these verses have to say about taking risks? How is risk-taking necessary if we're going to take advantage of the opportunities God has for us?

Answering God's call and being a follower of Christ requires us to take risks. If we give in to fear and avoid challenges, we'll miss out on the opportunities that God has in store for us.

Desperate to Please (10 minutes)

Supplies: Bibles, electronic devices with Internet access

From *Unafraid*, by Adam Hamilton

If you allow your fear of disappointing others and your fear of criticism to control you, you'll struggle to operate any kind of business, to offer any kinds of goods or services, or to provide any kind of leadership at all. Why? Because no matter what you do, you will disappoint someone.

Discuss:

- Where in your life do you feel the most pressure to please others?
- What would you say affects you more—praise or criticism? Why?

Divide into teams of three or four. Make sure that at least one person in each group has an electronic device that can access the Internet. As a team, come up with a book, restaurant, television show, song, or movie that everyone in the team agrees is very good. Once you're in agreement, find online reviews of it. (You can find these at Amazon, Rotten Tomatoes, iTunes, Yelp, or another popular app or website.)

Find one or more negative reviews. For each negative review you read, discuss:

- Does the reviewer make any points that you agree with?
- What criticism in the review seems completely unfair or uncalled for?
- Do you think the artists or management behind the products you chose could benefit from reading any of these negative reviews?
- What parts of the reviews do you think are not helpful and would only discourage the people behind these products?
- How would our world be different if people let the fear of failure keep them from trying new things or creating new products?

Read aloud Romans 8:31-39. Discuss:

- What do these verses, from Paul's letter to the Romans, have to say about fear of failure?
- Why, according to Paul, should we not fear people who "condemn" us?
- How might these verses give you hope when you face criticism, ridicule, or fear of failure?

It's OK for people to have different opinions. Few, if any, products or restaurants or movies are universally loved. And there are plenty of occasions when criticism is justified. But fear of failure and rejection can keep us from becoming the people God calls us to be and doing the work that God has set out for us.

Meaning Matters (10 minutes)

Supplies: Bibles, paper, pens or pencils

From *Unafraid*, by Adam Hamilton

We can fear that our lives will have been insignificant or meaningless unless we accomplish something big. But that is a false fear. Clearly, few people accomplish something truly "big" with their lives—and it is not the "big" thing that will ensure that our lives have meaning. Rather, the sum total of hundreds and thousands of small acts that we do across the course of our lives is what truly gives our lives meaning. "Small things done with great love will change the world" is commonly cited as Saint Teresa of Calcutta's words to live by.

Read aloud Matthew 22:34-40. Discuss:

- What does Jesus teach is the greatest commandment? (He is citing Deuteronomy 6:5.)
- What does Jesus tell us is the second greatest commandment? (He is citing the second half of Leviticus 19:18.)

Adam Hamilton, in *Unafraid*, explains that we don't necessarily have to do "great" things in order to follow these great commandments. Often we show our love for God and neighbor through little things.

Divide into teams of three or four. Each team should brainstorm two lists: one of little ways that we can or do show love to God on a daily basis, and one of little ways that we can or do show love to our neighbors on a daily basis.

These can be ways that we directly express our love (such as through prayer to God or giving food to someone who is hungry). These can also be ways that are indirect (such as showing our love to God by obeying God's commandments or showing love for neighbors by conserving resources such as water that may be scarce in some parts of the world).

Spend four minutes working on your lists, and then invite each team to read aloud its lists. Then discuss:

- Which of these things that you listed do you already do (or make an effort to do)?
- Which of these things could you start doing? Which could you make a habit of doing?

Many of us aspire to do great things—things that will be recognized and remembered and make a big impact. Discuss:

- On a scale of 0 through 10—where 0 is "not at all" and 10 is "very much"—how important is it to you to do something great or memorable with your life?
- On a scale of 0 through 10, how much do you fear not doing something great or memorable?

It's important to remember that God calls all of us to devote ourselves to the work of God's kingdom and to the love of God and neighbor. But relatively few people will be able to answer this call in ways that are widely recognized and regarded as great. Many people live out Jesus' "great" commandments in ways that go unnoticed. Read aloud Matthew 6:1-6. Discuss:

- What should our attitude be when it comes to how we show love to God and others?
- What do these verses have to say about the pressure we feel to be great?
- A famous saying, often attributed to Saint Teresa, says, "Small things done with great love will change the world." What are

some ways in which "small things"—actions that go unnoticed—can make a great impact?

Many people aspire to be great. But it's important for us to remember that greatness doesn't necessarily involve big accomplishments. More often than not, people express their greatness through small, day-to-day actions that go unnoticed.

Alone and Unloved (10 minutes)

Supplies: Bibles, notecards, pens or pencils

> ### From *Unafraid*, by Adam Hamilton
> This is what church is supposed to look like: not just people worshipping together, but people in relationships who are volunteering together, growing together, studying together, and playing together—just doing life together in a vibrant web of community.

Read aloud Mark 2:1-12. Discuss:

- How would this story have been different if the paralyzed man had not been with his friends?
- Whose faith does Jesus commend in verse 5?

Once again, divide into teams of three or four. Each team should create a story about a current-day situation in which a group of friends shows extraordinary faith by going out of their way to help a friend. Allow a few minutes for teams to create and discuss the story.

Adam Hamilton says, "In a very real sense, the entire New Testament can be read as an instruction manual for how to live together in Christian community." Discuss:

- What does the story of the four friends of the paralytic, as well as the stories we came up with, teach us about what it means to be a Christian community?

- How do people in our congregation and youth ministry show the faith and commitment that we see in these stories?

- How could our congregation or youth ministry do a better job of living out Jesus' instructions for being a Christian community? How could we do a better job of showing one another faith and compassion?

One of the most common fears that people struggle with is the fear of being alone or unloved. God calls us to be people who take away these fears—people from whom others can expect love and companionship.

Take a minute to set a personal goal for the week when it comes to being a friend to others. Though you can't predict when you'll need to cut a hole in the roof and lower someone into a crowded room, you can be intentional about getting to know a new person, performing an act of kindness for a stranger, or going out of your way to let people know they are appreciated.

Whatever goal you choose should be something specific that you can accomplish in the next week. Write down your goal for the week on a notecard or small sheet of paper that you can keep in your wallet, purse, backpack, or Bible. Share your goal with a partner or with your team so you can hold one another accountable for meeting your goals.

Closing (5 minutes)

From *Unafraid*, by Adam Hamilton

You can harness the power of your imagination to conjure up a future in which you are alone and unloved. Or you can use that same power to imagine the truth of the scriptures that say that there is a God who knows you, who loves you, and who is always by your side. You are loved with a love that will not let you go.

Close your time together by discussing the following questions:

- What is one thing that you learned or that you will think about differently as a result of today's session?
- What is one thing that you will do this week in response to what you've learned or discussed today?

Close with the prayer below or one of your own:

God, thank you for this time we've had together today. We know that, because of you, we are never alone or unloved. Show us in the coming week how we can be people of love, encouragement, and compassion so that we can create a community where no one lives in fear of failure, disappointment, or loneliness. Amen.

4

APOCALYPSE, CHANGE, MISSING OUT, AND FINANCES

When you first read the title of this session, it may appear to be a list of four completely unrelated things. Like other topics we've covered in this study, these are things that people often fear. More specifically, they're things that we fear when we forget who is in control.

We often live with the illusion that we are in control, that we know what we need, and that we can provide for ourselves. When we face realities that destroy this illusion—when change is forced on us, when political or economic factors threaten our way of life, when we miss out on something that is important to us—we become susceptible to fear and anxiety.

The good news is that we are children of a God who loves us and provides for us and who has control over all things. When we focus on God's will instead of our desires and when we put our full trust in God's plan, we can overcome fear and stress and live as the people God calls us to be.

This session corresponds to the following chapters in *Unafraid* by Adam Hamilton:

- Chapter 13: A Dystopian Future
- Chapter 14: We Never Did It That Way Before
- Chapter 15: FOMO
- Chapter 16: I Could Buy Me a Boat

Session Activities

Opening: Hopes and Fears (5–10 minutes)

Supplies: whiteboard or paper, markers

From *Unafraid*, by Adam Hamilton

Though paradise was lost in the opening chapters of the Bible, the Bible ends with paradise restored. In the end, God, goodness, love, and life will ultimately prevail, even if, for a time, evil, destruction, and death seem to have the upper hand.

As you did in the opening session, begin your time together by sharing hopes and fears. Again, list these hopes and fears on a whiteboard or large sheet of paper.

Also use this time to discuss your commitment from the "Alone and Unloved" activity in the previous session. This involved being intentional about being a friend to others during the past week. Talk about how you were successful and what challenges you faced. Discuss:

- Based on the quote above from Adam Hamilton, what do you think might we be talking about during this session?

Then open your time together with this prayer or one of your own:

God, thank you again for this opportunity to gather together and reflect on the message you have for us. Open our hearts and minds so that we are able to let go of our fears and prejudices and see people through your eyes. As we discuss our fears and worries, remind us of the hope we have through you. Amen.

A Dystopian Future (10–15 minutes)

From *Unafraid*, by Adam Hamilton

In nearly every age, human beings have lived in dread of enemies, apocalyptic visions, and potential catastrophes that might come upon us, either from the gods, from the devil, from nature, or from our enemies. . . .

Living unafraid despite the possible dangers we face as a race does not require a $3 million investment in a luxury bomb shelter. It simply comes down to our acronym:

Face your fears with faith.
Examine your assumptions in the light of the facts.
Attack your anxieties with action.
Release your cares to God.

Adam Hamilton devotes a chapter of *Unafraid* to the topic of "dystopia." A dystopia is the opposite of a utopia. It is a nation or land where an effort to create a better or perfect society has resulted in oppression or dysfunction. Most dystopias involve authoritarian regimes, and many involve overbearing technology. Dystopian stories have long had an impact on our culture. You may have read the dystopian novels *1984* or *Brave New World* in school; or you may be familiar with popular dystopian series such as *The Hunger Games* and *Divergent*. Discuss:

- Are you familiar with the term "dystopia"? How would you describe a dystopia?

43

- Have you read dystopian novels such as *1984, Brave New World,* or *The Hunger Games*? What do these works of fiction say about our world and what it could become?
- What other works of fiction (books, movies, television shows, comics, and so forth) are you familiar with that present a dystopian view of the future?
- Which dystopian vision of the future do you find most realistic? Which strike you as completely unrealistic? Which worry you the most? Why?

Divide into teams of three or four. Each team should imagine a dystopian future that seems possible based on something in our present-day world. Usually when writers create a dystopia, they envision what might happen if something currently going on is allowed to continue and grow. Many dystopias involve misusing or overusing certain technologies. Others involve taking away freedom and human rights.

Take a few minutes to imagine your dystopias, then allow each team to present what it came up with. For each dystopia, discuss:

- How likely do you think it is that this dystopia could become a reality?
- How much do you fear this dystopian vision becoming a reality?

The dystopias that have the biggest impact are those that seem most realistic. Many who have read *1984* become understandably nervous whenever elected leaders overstep their authority or when a large tech company invades the privacy of its users. At their best, dystopian novels and movies make us cautious; but if we're not careful, they can also make us afraid. Discuss:

- What is the difference between being cautious and being afraid?

Look back at the FEAR acronym that Adam Hamilton suggests as a way to respond when things take a turn for the worse. Discuss:

- How does Hamilton's acronym give us a way to respond when we see some of our dystopian visions becoming a reality? How can we face and examine our fears so we can respond with action and give our worries to God?

We will always be faced with political, economic, environmental, and technological realities that are beyond our control. But God gives us the tools to face these realities with faith, to respond by putting our faith into action, and to give our worries over to God.

We Never Did It That Way Before (10 minutes)

Supplies: Bibles

From *Unafraid*, by Adam Hamilton

Human beings are change-averse. The fear of change keeps some people in miserable marriages, and … motivates some to stay in jobs they can't stand. … The Egyptian human rights activist Amr Hamzawy said that the fear of change kept millions in the Arab world living under authoritarian regimes.

Discuss:

- When in your life have you been afraid or upset because something changed? Looking back, do you think your fear or frustration was justified?
- When, if ever, have you continued to do something you shouldn't have because you were afraid of change?
- For what reasons do you think people fear change?

One of the best-known stories from the Scriptures is the Israelites' escape from slavery in Egypt and journey toward the Promised Land. The Israelites encountered all sorts of challenges along this journey, and a trip that should have taken weeks or months ended up lasting forty years. During this difficult time, God provided for the people of Israel, giving them food and water in a desert environment that didn't have much to offer, guiding them along their path to their new home, and empowering them to prevail over their enemies.

Read aloud the following Scriptures:

- Numbers 11:4-6 ("Manna" was a special type of bread that God had given to the Israelites when they'd been hungry in the desert.)
- Numbers 13:25–14:4 (Twelve Israelite spies had explored the Promised Land and reported back on what they had found.)

Discuss:

- What attitude do the Israelites have about their journey to the Promised Land?
- Why do you think they would consider returning to slavery in Egypt?
- When in your life have you felt like the Israelites? When have you wanted to quit instead of moving forward with something new and challenging?

The Israelites who complained never made it to the Promised Land, but their children did. And their descendants would enjoy God's blessing and protection for many centuries. But a fear of change nearly brought the long and glorious story of God's people to an early end.

FOMO (15 minutes)

From *Unafraid*, by Adam Hamilton
FOMO, or the fear of missing out ... [is] the longing not only for the material things your neighbors own but to do whatever seemingly pleasurable or fashionable thing they are doing.

Discuss:

- Are you familiar with the concept of FOMO or the fear of missing out?

- When have you been afraid of missing out on something?
  (This could involve not being invited to a party or gathering,
  not being selected to play on a team or go on a trip, or not being
  able to participate in an activity.)
- When have you become upset because you had missed out on
  something (perhaps something that your friends kept talking
  about or posting pictures of)?

Divide into teams of three or four. Each team should prepare a skit
involving someone who misses out on something that would have been
enjoyable or rewarding. Every member of the team should play a role. One
person should play the role of the person who missed out; the others should
talk about or refer to the opportunity that the person missed out on.

Teams should imagine how the characters would respond in such a
situation. Would the person who missed out be polite? Would the person
avoid talking about what had been missed out on? Would the person be
angry? What about the others? Would they try not to bring up the situation,
or would they rub it in the face of the person who missed out?

Allow teams only a few minutes to come up with their skits. (Teams need
only to come up with the basic story; the rest can be improvised.) Then have
each team present its skit. Discuss:

- Which of these skits do you relate to the most?
- How did the fear of missing out have a negative effect on the
  characters in these skits?

Read aloud Ecclesiastes 2:4-11. Discuss:

- What does the writer of these verses have to say about his projects
  and accomplishments?
- Why did he decide that all his properties, possessions, and
  achievements were meaningless?
- How do these verses relate to the fear of missing out?

Most everyone struggles with a fear of missing out. We see what other people have and what they are doing, and we become jealous or worry that these opportunities will not be available to us. But this fear is the result of focusing on our desires instead of on God's will for us.

I Could Buy Me a Boat (10 minutes)

Supplies: Bibles, notecards, pens or pencils

> ### From *Unafraid*, by Adam Hamilton
>
> According to a recent survey conducted by the American Psychological Association, money is the number one source of stress for Americans. This is true not only for lower-income people but also for middle-income and, perhaps surprisingly, high-income people. Even millionaires worry about financial security.

Read aloud the quote above. Discuss:

- On a scale from 0 to 10, with 0 being "not at all" and 10 being "entirely," how surprised are you that money is the top source of stress for Americans—even those who are millionaires?
- Why do you think money is such a source of stress, even for people who have a lot of it?

Adam Hamilton, in this chapter of *Unafraid*, mentions a country song by Chris Janson called "Buy Me a Boat." The song humorously makes the point that money can't buy everything and can't solve all of our problems, but it can buy us a boat and a truck and a trailer and a Yeti cooler.

Often we take the same approach to money as Chris Janson in his song. We know that money can't buy us happiness and fulfillment, but it can buy us things that we feel we need in order to be happy and fulfilled.

In the space on the following page, make a list of things that, at one time or another in your life, you needed to have even though they weren't really a necessity. (Maybe you needed a certain pair of shoes or a phone or a particular video game.) Spend a couple of minutes making your list.

Then go around the room and have each person name the item on his or her list that seems most ridiculous in retrospect. Discuss:

- Why do we sometimes feel we need things that we really don't need?

Read aloud Matthew 6:25-34. Discuss:

- What do these verses tell us about what we actually need?
- Why does Jesus in these verses tell us not to worry?
- Jesus tells us that we can trust God to provide for needs such as food and clothing. In what ways does God provide for these needs for us?
- When, if ever, has it been difficult for you to trust in God's promise to provide for your needs?

Take a couple of minutes to reflect on what you truly need, what God has provided for you, and what you sometimes think you need. Identify one thing that you sometimes think you need but could actually do without. Commit, during the coming week, to go without this thing. The thing you might go without may include a snack or drink that you buy almost every day, a video game that you've been obsessed with, or a social media application that you feel is necessary for communication.

Find a partner and tell that person the commitment you're making. Hold one another accountable to your commitments during the week, checking in with each other every two or three days.

Money and possessions are often a source of stress because we allow them to be. As followers of Christ, we must trust God to provide for us.

Closing (5 minutes)

From *Unafraid*, by Adam Hamilton
Look for the blessings in your own life, giving thanks for what you have. Worship God in word and deed, and you'll already be experiencing what Saint Paul calls "the life that really is life."

Close your time together by discussing the following questions:

- What is one thing that you learned or that you will think about differently as a result of today's session?
- What is one thing that you will do this week in response to what you've learned or discussed today?
- Read the quote above from *Unafraid* by Adam Hamilton. What does this quote have to do with what we've learned and discussed today?

Close with the prayer below or one of your own:

God, thank you for this opportunity to learn from one another and from you. In the days and weeks to come, make us aware of the blessings in our lives, especially when we tend to focus on what others have or what we might be missing out on. We know that you love us and provide for us. Give us the wisdom and strength to deal with our fears. In Jesus' name we pray. Amen.

5

AGING, ILLNESS, DYING, AND FEAR OF THE LORD

No matter how young and healthy we are, one day we all will face the realities of aging and death. The knowledge that we will grow old and die is a source of fear and stress for many people. But God offers us eternal life in Christ and promises that our temporary, frail bodies will be replaced with perfect, indestructible bodies.

This truth, that God has overcome death and we will, too, should inspire us to live as people of hope. We can face any fear knowing that God's love and power will have the final say. And we can live our lives in a way that shows other people how God's promises are at work in us.

This session corresponds to the following chapters in *Unafraid* by Adam Hamilton:

- Chapter 17: "I Don't Want to Grow Old!"
- Chapter 18: Anxiety, Worry, and Physical Illness
- Chapter 19: "I'm Not Ready to Die"
- Chapter 20: Living with Fear, yet Unafraid

Session Activities

Opening: Hopes and Fears (5–10 minutes)

Supplies: whiteboard or paper, markers

From *Unafraid*, by Adam Hamilton

All of us have moments when we struggle with anxiety about growing old, getting sick, and dying. Perhaps you've known the feeling of anxiety—a feeling like you can't breathe—when contemplating these same concerns.

As you did in previous sessions, begin your time together by sharing hopes and fears. Again, list these hopes and fears on a whiteboard or large sheet of paper.

Also use this time to discuss your commitment from the "I Could Buy Me a Boat" activity in the previous session. This involved giving up something this past week that you didn't really need. Talk about how you were successful and what challenges you faced. Discuss:

- Based on the quote above from Adam Hamilton, what do you think we might be talking about during this session?

Then open your time together with this prayer or one of your own:

God, thank you for bringing us back together for this final session. Watch over us as we continue to reflect on our fears and anxieties. Open our eyes, ears, and minds to the message you have for us, and show us the hope that can overcome any fear we encounter. Amen.

"I Don't Want to Grow Old!" (15 minutes)

Supplies: slips of paper, pens or pencils

From *Unafraid*, by Adam Hamilton

Most of us fear growing old and leaving behind the life stage we're currently in. ... Yet, what I've found to be true in my life, and in the lives of most of the people I know, is that each stage of life (with a few momentary exceptions) has been better than the one before. And that is precisely what nearly every study on aging shows.

Write on a slip of paper the age that you would consider "old." After writing this age, fold your slip of paper.

One person should collect everyone's slips of paper, unfold them, and read them aloud one at a time. If time permits, find the median or mean of these ages and see if there are any outliers. Discuss:

- Was your idea of old age consistent with other people's (or with the group average)?
- On a scale from 0 to 10, where 0 is "not at all" and 10 is "all the time," how much do you worry about aging?
- On a scale from 0 to 10, where 0 is "completely disagree" and 10 is "completely agree," how much do you agree or disagree with this statement: "Our culture celebrates youth and teaches us to fear getting older"?
- How does our culture teach us that we should dread and resist getting older? (Think particularly of products that are designed to make people look and feel younger.)

Divide into teams of three or four. Your team should come up with a product designed for people who are worried about aging. This product should promise to slow or stop some part of the aging process and to keep its users looking or feeling young. Spend a few minutes coming up with an idea. Then each team should pitch its idea. Talk about how your product ideas are similar to products already being sold and advertised.

Adam Hamilton, in *Unafraid*, notes that, while we often get the impression that we should fear and resist aging, studies show that people in their sixties and seventies are happier than those in their twenties and thirties.

Hamilton lists the following reasons why people become happier in their old age:

- They have more reasonable expectations.
- They are more appreciative of what they have.
- They have more time to spend with family and friends.
- They tend to have time for hobbies, travel, and other leisure activities.
- They feel less pressure and stress to meet others' expectations.
- They tend to have fewer negative and more positive emotions.
- The breadth of their life experiences leads them to be less overwhelmed by adversity.

Discuss:

- Which of these reasons surprise you?
- Which make the most sense?
- For what other reasons might older people be happier than younger people?
- Do these reasons change your thoughts on aging? If so, how?
- How should our Christian faith affect our attitudes toward aging?

Though many people are inclined to dread and resist getting older, maybe we should embrace it. There are definitely things that we lose as we age, but it's possible that we will gain far more.

Anxiety, Worry, and Physical Illness (5–10 minutes)

From *Unafraid*, by Adam Hamilton

Worry and anxiety accomplish *nothing,* but we can do *something.* We can choose a better way.

Read aloud Philippians 4:4-7. Discuss:

- Verse 6 says that we should not worry. What does it mean to worry? What comes to mind when you think of worrying?
- When do you worry the most?
- How do you deal with your worry?

Adam Hamilton, in *Unafraid*, says that the best way to address our worry is through "mindfulness." Mindfulness involves not dwelling on the future and what *could* or *might* happen but instead focusing on the joy that we have in our lives right now, particularly the joy that we have in our relationships. Discuss:

- When have you allowed the fear of what could or might happen to keep you from enjoying life in the moment?
- How has worry had a negative effect on your relationships with God and others?

Think about the week ahead. Instead of dwelling on the things about the coming week that worry you or stress you out, reflect on the blessings that you will enjoy this week. These could include people whom you get to talk to and spend time with, opportunities you have to learn or to do things that you enjoy, or chances you have to worship God and show God's love to other people. Make a list of these blessings in the space below.

Everyone worries. We won't be able to avoid worry and stress, but we don't have to let our worries control us, and we must not allow fear of the future to keep us from enjoying blessings and relationships in the present.

"I'm Not Ready to Die" (10 minutes)

Supplies: Bibles

From *Unafraid,* by Adam Hamilton
Christianity proclaims that God's response to our fear of death is the death and resurrection of Christ. Through his death and resurrection Jesus conquered death. His resurrection leads us to say that evil, illness, sin, and death will never have the final word. There is always hope.

Have participants stand and gather in the middle of the room. One person should have a copy of this book and should read aloud each of the statements below. The other participants should move to one end of the room or the other end to indicate how strongly they agree or disagree with each statement. (One wall of the room should represent "strongly agree." The opposite wall should represent "strongly disagree.")

Following each statement, participants should explain why they chose to stand where they did. The statements are:

1. Because we will all die one day, we should not worry about death.
2. Because God has promised us eternal life through Christ, we should not be afraid of death.
3. Because we look forward to eternal life, we shouldn't worry about this life or this world.

Death is a topic that people often feel uncomfortable discussing. Most of us don't like to think about our own death, even though it is inevitable and even though almost nothing in our lives is more painful than the death of a loved one. But we also know that death does not have the final say and that God promises us eternal life in a new and perfect body.

Read aloud each of the passages of Scripture below. For each one discuss:

- What does this Scripture tell us about death or God's promise of eternal life?
- How does this Scripture give us hope when we fear death?

Scriptures:

- John 11:25-26
- John 14:1-3
- 1 Corinthians 15:50-58
- 2 Corinthians 4:16-18

We have a promise of eternal life beyond death. How does this promise affect our lives here and now? Some Christians have taken the promise as a reason not to worry about the problems facing the world we live in now. After all, if we know that we'll eventually live forever in a perfect world with a perfect body, why should we spend time and energy on a life and world that are only temporary? Yet, Jesus teaches us that our actions in this life matter. Discuss:

- Why should we be concerned with this life when we know that God has promised us eternal life?
- One reason it's important to be concerned with this life is because we have a chance to give people a glimpse of God's eternal kingdom. How can our actions in this life give people hope for what is to come?

We must all face the reality of death. But, because of Christ, we can face this reality with hope, and we can pass along this hope to a fearful world.

Living With Fear, yet Unafraid (10 minutes)

From *Unafraid*, by Adam Hamilton

We've seen that our capacity to fear is a gift meant to help us, protect us, and motivate us. The challenge comes when we fear things that are not threats or we exaggerate in our minds the magnitude of the threat or the odds that it will affect us. When we become fear-full, that which was intended to protect us ends up controlling us and robbing us of a full life.

Living unafraid, then, is not to live without fear; it is to live without being controlled and consumed by fear.

Read aloud the quotation above. Discuss:

- When can fear be a good thing? How can it motivate and protect you?
- What do you think it means to be "controlled and consumed by fear"?

In the space that follows on the next page, make two lists.

The first list should be a list of good fear—ways in which fear can keep you safe or inspire you to grow and improve. (For instance, because of a fear of drowning you only swim in areas that are supervised by a lifeguard.)

The second list should be a list of bad fear—ways that fear can cause us to do things that are harmful to ourselves or others. (For instance, a fear of terrorism may cause you to be suspicious of people of certain ethnic or religious groups.)

It is OK if some items are humorous. ("Fear of heights protects me from giving in to the urge to try to long jump across the Grand Canyon.") And it's quite possible that one fear could be on both lists. (Fear of failure might motivate you to set goals and work hard to reach them; it also might cause you to become resentful toward those who seem to be more successful than you.)

Good Fear   **Bad Fear**

After you've had a few minutes to work on your lists, invite participants to read aloud one or more items from their list.

There is one fear that is always productive. Read aloud each of the following Scriptures from the Book of Proverbs. (Have a different participant read aloud each Scripture.)

- Proverbs 1:7
- Proverbs 10:27
- Proverbs 14:26-27

Discuss:

- What fear is mentioned in each of these Scriptures?
- What do you think it means to fear God?

Many Christians over the centuries have interpreted the fear of God as the fear of God's wrath and punishment. But this fear may be better understood as awe, reverence, or respect. We recognize that God is great and holy, that God controls all things, and that God has high standards and expectations for us. If we have a healthy fear of God, we will not be "controlled and consumed" by other fears but will be free to live full lives as God's people.

Closing (5 minutes)

From *Unafraid*, by Adam Hamilton

You and I will experience fear, but we don't have to be oppressed, defeated, or controlled by it. We can face our fears with faith, examine our assumptions in light of facts, attack our anxieties with action, and release our cares to God. And in doing this we will discover the "peace of God that exceeds all understanding." This peace allows us to live unafraid with courage and hope.

Close your time together by discussing the following questions:

- What is one thing that you learned or that you will think about differently as a result of today's session?
- What is one thing that you will do this week in response to what you've learned or discussed today?

Read the quote above from *Unafraid* by Adam Hamilton. Jot down this quote on a scrap of paper that you can keep in a wallet or purse, or snap a picture of it with your phone. Look back on this quote as a reminder of what you have learned over the course of this study and as inspiration to live "unafraid with courage and hope."

Close with the prayer below or one of your own:

God, thank you for the time we've had together over the past several weeks and this opportunity we've had to reflect on fear. Give us the courage to face our fears knowing that you are in control of all things. And guide us so that others can see the hope we have in you. We pray these things in Jesus' name. Amen.

www.ingramcontent.com/pod-product-compliance
Lightning Source LLC
Chambersburg PA
CBHW070906100426
42737CB00047B/2963